ABOUT THE AUTHOR

Kat Lyons is a Queer Bristol-based writer and performer whose work is grounded in everyday politics and a love of storytelling. They facilitate creative writing workshops for all ages and have performed around the UK at theatres, poetry nights and places such as WOMAD, Shambala and The Eden Project. Kat has presented at the University of South Wales Storytelling Symposium, been published in journals including Bath Magg and Under the Radar, commissioned by The Arts Institute Plymouth, and nominated for the Jerwood Poetry in Performance Award. As well as co-hosting spoken word nights with Raise the Bar, Kat is the producer and host of SpitFire, a series of poetry events designed to platform older women's voices. At the time of writing, Kat is touring Dry Season, their solo spoken word theatre show exploring gender, age and menopause. Love Beneath the Nails is their debut poetry collection.

www.katlyons.co.uk
@Words_and_weeds
katlyonsartist@gmail.com

Kat Lyons
love beneath the nails

VERVE
POETRY PRESS
BIRMINGHAM

PUBLISHED BY VERVE POETRY PRESS
https://vervepoetrypress.com
mail@vervepoetrypress.com

FIRST PUBLISHED FEB 2022

Printed and bound in the UK
by ImprintDigital, Exeter

ISBN: 978-1-913917-03-6

This book is dedicated to mum (I wish you could be here) and dad (I'm so glad you are). Thank you for filling my childhood with songs and books and bedtime stories. Yes, I was often reading under the duvet when I should have been sleeping, but I hope you'll agree it was worth it.

CONTENTS

painted

dry season

Introduction/ Notes on the text

Notes & Acknowledgements

love beneath the nails

'one angle blunts, another sharpens'
- Jane Hirshfield, *stone and knife*

broken

after the funeral

january

my grief and i come home. we eat toast
and peanut butter for the protein
drink tea and boil the kettle dry.
we are scolded by the steam. we sit
on the sofa which is too small for both of us.
i read; grief fidgets
until i stop.

april

i take my grief to the park. the field is mud
the mud is licked with bright new grassy tongues.
in the ornamental bed we kneel among crocuses.
i plant my fingers, whisper *tell me how it feels*
to root, to hide a portion of yourself inside the earth.

june

on weekends we go walking to the river.
our kicked stones cause ripples. our tongues turn
minnows into whales.
my grief points out the kingfisher; a brief blue lantern
flashing like a siren
or a lighthouse.

august

i take my grief to the beach and leave it
huddled on the blanket with my clothes.
breath locked behind my teeth
i count down into mute submersion, waiting to be
rolled between the palms of sea and sky.

november

my grief comes down to the harbourside. we play
which boat is mine? - i want them all, imagine
bite-sized mornings delivered through portholes.
when we leave, i'll take the helm while grief casts off.
it's good at ropes and knots - the making, the undoing.

january

my grief grows shabby, edges smoothed by touch. eventually
it fits in my back pocket. this curled up, sharp-toothed stub.
i try to remember
to check before sitting down.
am pockmarked from the moments
i forget.

fallow

since her death, the weeds have grown
brave. hold your brother's hand
small again, clutching mittens in a crowd.

shiver in adult clothes.
scuff big-girl shoes in the dirt, watch
your mother's house stripped. don't think

of novels drowning in the pulping vat.
order disappointed pizza, drink the last of her
good wine from plastic mugs, sleep on

camping mats. possessions only weigh you down.
platitudes beneath your feet
like upturned lego bricks.

load plants and oddments, bubble-wrap her laugh
dig out the remains of last night's pizza.
eat it in a layby halfway home.

self-examination

once a month i look
for changes   chunks in the jellybag
lumps in the roux

i knead my flesh
drag my thoughts up keep my eyes
fixed   the yellowed plant above the bath
throws out optimistic runners tiny fists of roots

she checked herself
she wore rose pink she loved
her garden   they painted her in
desert colours blood and iodine

i lift and squeeze
before the mirror   she always wanted more
cleavage grew a cup size
under reconstruction

on holiday she undressed
in our shared room   she lost her nipples
she still looked great in a fitted jumper

who touched her last, netted her breath
shivered her world into bright splinters
lifted the weight from her chest?

sometimes i sleep
arms crossed palms cupped
holding myself in place.

she dreams of lighthouses

their yellow eyes. blink
turn. screw-top heads

perched sentinel. watch
for shuttered lanterns and safe waters. wait

for the snag, to be landed, laid -
cured by sunlight. curious hands on her

stitches, frayed seams and knots
revealed. a fairground mermaid.

monkey sewn to fishtail. scales
drying to dulled inconsequence.

cavity

i brush my teeth in the bathroom i am an adult and this is what
we do we have clean teeth that speak of routines that shine
with organisation so i brush my teeth for two minutes after
breakfast and before bed i time it with a stopwatch on my
phone i am still not responsible enough i brush my teeth
and use a special plastic stick in the crevices where dirt hides
morning and evening i brush between meals i brush after snacks
i brush between those times i've learnt fractions are infinite
anything can be split with a thin enough wedge i brush my teeth
in a repetitive circular motion with my toothbrush held at a
45-degree angle to my gums just like the leaflets advise i buy a
protractor to measure the angle precision is important health is
a serious business i am told this by serious men i brush my teeth
and every time i pass a mirror i peel my lips back like a nervous
mare do they shine yet? it's hard to see beneath the blood but i
imagine they're glowing i brush my teeth and check my progress
in reflective surfaces my swollen face wallows in spoon bellies
peers up at me from puddles before the red drops shake it free i
brush and brush and in-between i practice saying serious things
with my raw mouth it's hard to fit the words around my tongue
grown thick with adulthood my throat crammed with vitamins
and ballpoint pens and magnetic whiteboards and packs of nail
files and plastic-free razors and spare chargers for electrical
devices and spf30 even on cloudy days and labelled boxes of
leftovers in the freezer and much more economic in the long-
run people don't understand what i'm saying i am choking i have
worn away my voice to pristine silence i have worn away the
bristles and my gums but still i brush and when i bite down now
with what were teeth the whole world tastes of iron and gleams

blunt edges cause more injuries

in the white gloss bathroom of my rented house
i cut.

i use her good fabric scissors. i never learnt
to sew. i bury her

wicker workbox beneath my bed. avoid
the needles' prying eyes.

she used the right tool for every job.
i trust the edge of anyone dressed as a knife.

i prime my surfaces, keep my blades
sharp. her cheekbones surface in my face.

we kneel before the mirror.
bare our necks.

the first year

is nearly over. unzip it like a shift dress
shrug it off, let it fall.
it is too small for you now.
when it puddles around your feet
tread water. you are still

soft. some days
peel easily, others swaddle you.
use your teeth - this will not be pretty but
we do what we must. you will

pick stray minutes from your fingernails
for months. in bed with a new lover
you will shift uneasily. stale crumbs of memories
prick beneath the sheets. the weight of love

is measured out in salt. swim
through silt and brine, inhale
as it fills your throat. trust evaporation.
time and light will crystalize you too.

bitten

a study in vertical perspective

during the lockdown we flattened
our gaze, drew the altar of our days
medieval style. icons front and centre.
importance indicated by size.

pets grew vast. nurses loomed like cloudbanks
hands raised in benediction or
farewell. three full moons climbed our roofs

we met through curtain cracks. we watched the sky
discard cerulean, cobalt, azure; dyed blue
as hospital scrubs, latex gloves, cheap disposable masks.

the galleries stayed dark. the gilded virgins kept on
hefting babies on their knees, cradling
the tender skulls of all the little gods.

my dad has a cough but we're not talking about that

we're talking about meat
and the supermarket order delivered to their door
and aren't they lucky

pick up the post with a litter-picker   snap
a photo for the family chatgroup
make a joke   laugh in pictograms

it can live on paper for two days
stick them in a box
it's not like they're important

move on   to what
he ate for dinner and his diy   i'm calling
every day now   he's scraping down

a bookcase   living-
room messy with uncradled words   he says
don't worry   it's only dust

llwyth dyn ei gorwgl (the load of a man is his coracle)

i'm running down
the towpath
with graveled breath
avoiding slipstreams
noting masks
turn
the dance of opposing
magnets now
even the air is not safe
there is always
a hawk somewhere
exploding something's present
into past tense
i've watched
strings of goslings vanish
jackdaws fall from nests
laid trembling
slippers of flesh
in straw-lined shoebox hospitals
come inevitable morning
the bird was gone
the manger
now a morgue
inside the box
a coracle
abandoned
on the riverside
another mile
moving in the pulse
my world pulls close

raindrops huddle on the leaves
the unseen raptor hunches
in the wood the wrens
sing up a storm

she opens her mouth to sing and the world jumps in

she's locked-down, playing ophelia.
her housemate, in on the game -

here, try this curtain
it looks just like her dress.

clutch plastic flowers, hide
razors, black mould, evidence. lie

still. quick
take a photo.

another body. another hundred
years of mad girls, nipples

hardening to knuckles
under sopping gauze, fingers splayed.

catch her
sinking into laughter. cutting loose

her flotsam. today
she'll rise from warm water.

close enough to touch

we stretch our fingers out. across the country
we are sleeping, or lying
awake in narrow childhood beds. we have returned
for a day or a week or just
too long. loitering
in late december's alleyway.
i fold myself into furniture
mindful of creases, observing

changes. new photos on the walls. dad climbs the stairs
slowly, on a new knee
which will never bend quite right.
we gift-wrap our lives
leave them
jumbled beneath the tree.
my framed smile looks down on me.
conversations are flavoured

by the sticky patina of years. time runs thick.
the dinner was delicious, but we've been eating leftovers
for two days now. we don't speak with our mouths
full. i want to say
i love you, and come away
clean and easy
as a knife from a new-baked cake. the timing perfect
that first cut barely visible.

the bear was first spotted on sunday evening

in an industrial area north-east of central norilsk.
her camouflage is useless here. she's starving
dirty cream and lost. a two-meter question mark
a mystery of wasted muscle.

google tells me the fur of ursus maritimus is transparent
and only looks white due to light-refracting particles
creating luminescence within each hair.
a healthy adult female can weigh 250kgs.
they are perfectly adapted to their environment
and are sometimes mistaken for snowdrifts.

she drags her mud-clogged paws across the road while
people take photographs.
it's hard to believe in things we can't touch but try it
she'll take your arm off.

three cars back in the traffic jam
a man has left his car. he stands
behind the open door, grey coat blending into grey
road.
it's risky, he could have watched her through the
windscreen
but maybe that's too much like tv.

she has wandered into a factory and remains
under observation. her condition is assessed.
she is despondent. her eyes are weeping.
it seems a reasonable response.

experts are flying in. i close the window
on my laptop. their helicopters
beat like moths against the glass. it's growing dark
and a polar bear is dying
in a russian factory, her dusty fur still scattering light.

when the bears came out of the arctic

they walked into the factories. we gave them jobs
we hated. they worked
in the freezers, the graveyard shifts. they were cost-effective.
they didn't need protective clothing.
they weren't interested in pensions.

they were granite in their strangeness. they smelt
of blood and salt and sky. when we passed on the street
we avoided their eyes. they kept to the bear lane
grew stained and pitted, wore down.
they took out their teeth.

now they slope in alleys, cadge a fag, suck on chips.
they've shrunk to fit. waning moons, heading towards
eclipse. watch them
shuffle under streetlights, hunch in cafeterias.
cry over the ice-cubes in a coke.

a process of decomposition

it didn't quite fit but fuck it
was beautiful and hands
always swell in summer

that quiet weight slipped from her
settled among eddying microbes nothing to
see not even a tan-line left

in the fumbling dark
rubber to the elbow like a vet
use enough sawdust you can deal with any mess

leave it three years and run
fingers through the dirt
smell it you'd never guess

there's still a diamond somewhere i suppose
we could have waited marked the barrel
sieved for it

there's a dead mouse in the bucket

you slipped and scrabbled in the night.
you swam and swam and swam and

drowned. yesterday i held
my breath and hoped to catch
a scrap of movement.

this morning i drink tea
drop my eyes
into shallow water.

maybe you climbed over our walls.
maybe you crept under our fences.

we were lucky
to find you before it became unpleasant
for us.

we discuss burial, the possibility
of smells, decide
not to bother.

we never touched you.
we washed our hands twice.

thoughts on forensic optography or, *image on her retina may show girl's slayer*

if we are not dead, how long do we keep
those images behind our eyes?
filed in the back room
in flipbooks, microfische carousels, zoetropes
in constant revolution. you can watch
if you come close enough.

in a world where this is true
dark glasses are worn in public at all times.
prisoners are refused this decency.
children are excused. i have heard
there are parties in the cities
where revelers go bare-eyed. we do not speak of them
in polite company.

opticians sign the official secrets act
before they strap their torches on
peer inside. our ancestors
wore mourning jewelry, their loved ones'
corneas preserved inside a locket, facing
the final optograph. they're much sought after
as curios. we store everything digitally now.

lovers exchange books of blank pages
to read before their weddings. they purify
their retinas, walk down the aisle blindfolded
beneath their veils, remove them
after the exchange of rings. this is the only time

they won't kiss
with their eyes shut.

vanishing point

remember the bugs? their bodies
smashed against our screens
the bloody smears the mess
they left

it's been a while
sometimes we look back
squint through arcs of viscera tonight
the roads are wet the air smells clean

we speed forward wipe aside
leaves weather minor inconveniences
guided by artificial eyes
follow our own reflected light to where

parallel lines converge tarmac hits
the horizon collides
with the star-crazed curve
of a sky as hard and clear as tempered glass

painted

the women in my pole-dance class

grind their hips
against their favourite tunes.
they stretch, emerge
from warm-up clothes with thighs and stomachs

bare. they leave their socks on
at first - it reduces friction.

watch them slide and thrust, their bodies
slip down the pole
oil slick. smiles
clipped by pressure: a woman's weight

against her flesh
her flesh against metal.

they concentrate
open their legs like books
spines bent back, hard hours
written in the precision of their limbs.

show me how to work
with gravity.

together, we kneel
on mottled shins. as winter squats
behind the door, crocus colours
bloom beneath our skin.

tell me it will stop hurting
eventually.

clench and twist
invert
dust the floor
with greying hair, come

down
in a raptor's glide.

#beatrice2018

*'...there is no one with a squeaky-clean past like brett
kavanaugh. he is an outstanding person and i'm
very honored to have chosen him."*
- president trump, 2018.

*'o god, that i were a man! i would eat his heart in
the marketplace.'*
- beatrice, act 4 scene 1. 'much ado about
nothing' by w. shakespeare.

(extract. interview under caution.)

i admit, it surprised
me too.
it's not my usual style.
i prefer the subtler approach - the pen
is mightier than the sword, you know?

not that i was ever allowed a sword.

yes. i have a sharp tongue
spit papercuts and yes
i use men as a whetstone but
can you blame me?
i hear them whispering behind my back
but never gossiping -
that's what women do.

men talk. their tone serious
their words hold weight
heavy enough
to sink a girl like stones.

our voices are light
our mouths dimmed switches.
unimportant speech
unrecorded history.

climb the ladder
of our spread legs.

i'm a bitch. i should put a tighter bridle
on my scold's tongue. honey
there's no need to get upset.

i used to be a cookie-cutter girl
gingerbread doll
everyone wanted a nibble. until i grew
up, out
too much for this
womanshape i lace myself into
every day. i collar my wild dog flesh
train my hair to sit
dip my tongue in sugar glaze, serve
on a newspaper platter.

lies slip
around our necks.

silence
becomes another stone.

yes. i confess
i caused a scene.

i ate his heart.

it tasted sweet.

when eve met isaac

they talked about apples, and the mechanics of falling.
examine the sheen on the ruddy skin, how it calls

your fingers. adjust your grip, they bruise easily.
their energy cannot be destroyed, but look

what happens when they tumble
how they lie spread, smashed into the dirt.

deflect the force, slap the ground and roll.
she learnt that in her self-

defense class. ignore the hiss. how they suck
their teeth at your body.

blame it on the hothouse weather.
walled gardens are always microclimates.

she packed her knowledge and left. he stayed
beneath the tree. the apples

cradled their maggots, swayed in the wind
waited for their chance.

what to wear when kissing girls on buses

a white shirt goes with anything. keep it
casual with the sleeves rolled up,
accessorise lightly, maybe a bold splash of colour

on the face. red's a popular choice -
a touch on the lips, don't be afraid
to go harder on the nose, the chin, the cheekbones

a playful splatter on the neck and down
the collar's open throat.
breasts visible, or not

enough -
you don't make the rules and you won't know till
later. your girlfriend cries

beside you on the bus.
her blood and yours, beating
a quiet applause on the floor.

practice the model strut: walk away
shoulders back, imagine a gold thread
pulling your head up, don't show

your nerves, your sweat. your fingers
slip from her hand. her hands
cover her face.

this summer's look is calcified. black eyes shuttered.
bone white shirts
buttoned over pulses.

component parts

the scar on my lover's throat is muted.
i never knew it fresh.
i walk my fingers back along the pale line
roll her shadowed footsteps up
out of the underpass.

my lover is a chef. she tells me
i need to understand, i can't just take
ingredients out, expect everything
to remain unchanged.
it's chemistry, she says.

five years ago beneath the bridge
the bottle is still
in his hand, glass teeth
unbroken. her skin
a stranger, moving closer.

this morning she brings down the axe, splits
oak into kindling
loads the burner with the acorn's dream.
we rake the ashes, build the fire again.
feed it splinters. coax it with another breath.

catcalled

1. *'look assertive'*

out on the public street in full possession of a body.
you lean on that wall like an ill-hung door.
you've no idea how you splinter
      bitch
slam
      pussy
shut
rattling between gateposts, wolf-
whistling through your empty keyhole, hinges
creaking
      baby
      baby
      baby.

2.   *'act and walk with confidence'*

he watches the women
the way they walk, the way they walk
past him. he is young and slight and easy to ignore
when silent. he fills his mouth with sweating words.
bark bigger little terrier, snap at shadows.
strangle yourself with your own short leash.

3. *'always be alert in your surroundings [...] don't use*
    earphones or handheld devices'

window-dressed for church, your face a closed shop.
twitch the curtains of your sunday suit
away from our clasped hands.
today we're *dirty pussyholes*, a display you want
to straighten. our passage disturbs
stale air around your tongue
your yellowed flypaper eyes.

4. *'stick to routes and forms of transport that others are using'*

car windows trail insults like roadkill guts.
at the unlit bus-stop we stand ankle-deep in entrails
grip our keys
use them to scrape off our shoes.
the rot is tracked across the pavement
crosshatched with women's footprints.
the smell gets in our hair. we hold our breath
cross the road. it follows us
all the way home.

5. *'avoid walking alone at night in places such as parks and side streets or any unfamiliar environment'*

in shorts in jeans in leggings in drag in a skirt in a raincoat
in a dress in heels in sandals in trainers in boots in a couple
in a group in an alley in a town in a car on a road on a
footpath on my own on my way to school to work to the
pub to the corner-shop to meet a friend to get a takeaway
to catch a bus to post a letter to exercise in the park in
spring summer autumn winter morning afternoon evening
twilight running walking sitting standing
still

a word in your ear

when *woman*
is gravel
in your shoe
sit down
hook it out
find
your limp is gone
your gimble pivots
horizons un-skew
your whiskers
come unglued
spring
out
you fit
through doorways
down alleyways
go
easy now
your corners
barely snag
on the curves
you loop in
ampersands
along your self-
mown path
a finger-width
of green
among the
brambles
a rabbit-

track
the barest
inch
of road
you'll take
a mile
at least
they tell you
don't
stray
out
in
no
man's
land

the trees are bloodied by the rising sun

manual labour

we learnt to count on our hands.
strung trust in cats-cradles

stuck out cautious tongues, tasted
easter-egg colours

painted on bitten quicks, our desire
still unhatched.

we ran out of fingers, tallying
the times we stuck them up

at passing cars, spine stiff.
knuckles jutted prows beneath our skin.

we used them to strike
a light, bring fire to our lips

stub cigarettes out on leech eyes
tip her head towards a kiss.

we refused
to wear our mittens. we grew

callouses. we learnt to pick the locks
and came to dinner uninvited

unscrubbed, palms
together in grace. see us now

spread on the table, grimed with life
love beneath the nails.

dry season

INTRODUCTION

Dry Season was written in response to my diagnosis and early experience of premature ovarian failure, following 18 months of undiagnosed symptoms including chronic insomnia, depression, and paranoid anxiety. As the initial shock wore off, I realised that my feelings of ignorance, shame and isolation were shared by countless others.

Taking into account factors such as race, class, ability, gender identity etc., women's experiences and voices aren't listened to as carefully, given as much weight or broadcast as loudly as men's. In the field of healthcare, studies repeatedly show that medical practitioners of all genders under-estimate and under-treat women's pain. Overall, women wait longer than men to receive treatment for the same complaints. When finally treated they are more likely to be offered psychological assistance or sedatives, while men are more likely to be offered medical treatment and anaesthetics. This dismissal of women's embodied experiences is especially evident within gynaecology, where people routinely wait years to be diagnosed with common, often debilitating conditions, such as endometriosis. Due to institutional and societal ageism older women's voices are especially muted, and in menopause-related issues, this combines with gender bias and misogyny to create a perfect storm of ignorance and repression[1].

Approximately 50% of humanity will experience menopause. Despite this some medical schools still don't include mandatory menopause education in their program, and many GPs are still unaware of the full spectrum of symptoms and treatment, and dismissive of those who come to them for help. The end result

---

[1] Not everyone who experiences menopause is a woman and institutional medical misogyny also affects those of other genders. The ongoing struggles of trans people to access necessary body-appropriate healthcare are well documented.

of all this is that an experience shared by half the UK population is widely seen as something embarrassing, shameful and either not fit to be mentioned at all, or if so, then only behind closed doors or as the butt of jokes.

Dry Season is my attempt to counter this and create more representation and open discussion of the issue, while at the same time letting loose and having a good old poetic bitch about the whole situation. I hope that by using my own journey as a lens through which to explore wider concerns, this piece will help generate knowledge and empathy between people of different ages, genders, and experiences. After all, while not everyone will go through menopause specifically, the process of aging and of accepting that transition is something we'll all have to learn. If we're lucky enough to get that far.

Finally, if you're having a hard time with this too, *Dry Season* is the proof that you're not alone. I see you. I hear you.
You can do this.

NOTES ON THE TEXT:

Italicised: stage instruction
Lx: stage instruction indicating a change in lighting
Fx: stage instruction indicating a change in soundscape

Pronouns etc:
Dry Season was written back in 2019 when I still identified (albeit tentatively) as a cis woman. Although this is not the case now, I decided not to retrospectively change the language in the script. That was me, then. In a few more years the period this story covers will probably feel too far away for me to perform it anyway. I will have shed more skin cells, grown more lines and become in many ways a different person, again.

welcome

wait. it is dark here in the theatre. settle into your seat and observe your rituals: check your sightlines, take a sip of the wine you bought at the theatre bar - overpriced admittedly but infused with atmosphere and somehow tasting much more exciting than the wine you drink at home.

watch. we are about to co-create an experience. we are about to time travel. i was 37 years old when this tale begins and by the time you read this who knows how many years will have passed. my remaining partially-working ovary may long ago have stuttered into silence. i may be 42 and still struggling, or 55 and out into the (hopefully) calmer waters beyond the perimenopausal surf but none of that matters right now, because together we will turn this small room into a portal.

listen. this was written for the breath and the air and the electric distance between your eyes and mine. it was written for the dust-motes drifting in the spotlight and settling on the floorboards of the stage, and for the energy encircling us both. it was designed to live in the moment and the audience but even pinned onto paper this artform cannot be stilled. trap it in a book and watch it squirm beneath the pages. relax and let it free, let it crawl up into your ears. oral literature is a grand tradition. we have been participating in storytelling ever since we first discovered we had tongues to speak and ears to listen and imaginations to carry us out beyond the firelight's edge and into other worlds.

so. are you sitting comfortably?
let me tell you a story.

*the curtains open. the stage is lit with a warm wash. there is a
projector screen on the back wall and a plain wooden desk and chair
mid-stage. there is a white angle-poise lamp on the desk. in front
of the lamp there is a large pump bottle of moisturiser, a remote-
control clicker for a projector, a small wind-up music box and a box of
prescription oestrogen gel. there are black storage boxes on the floor on
either side of the desk. there is nothing else on stage.*

1: are you sitting comfortably?

enter stage left. walk around to the front of the desk and sit on it. get comfortable. look up. face your audience. speak casually.

let me tell you a story. it's about a girl.

this girl has hair as pale as hay
and skin like fallen snow.
she has skin as dark as walnut juice
and hair black as a crow's wing.

sometimes she grows it long,
lets it down for princes to climb.
sometimes her hair, her long bright hair
her long bright too bright too beautiful hair
catches the eye and snags
on the thorns of powerful men.

sometimes she twists free.

sometimes she goes exploring.
she is uncharted territory.

she is the woodcutter's daughter
the millers' daughter
the merchant's daughter
the magician's daughter
the king's daughter

be honest - it doesn't really matter whose
daughter she is as long as she is accounted for.

she is so beautiful the stars want to
touch her.
she is plain but goodhearted
dutiful and pious
quick-witted and bold.
she will gamble away her birthright
shed her shining tail
walk on knives for a chance at love.

she is foolish and will not be told.

she wears dresses sewn with pearls
she wears her brothers' clothes
she veils her skin
but no matter what she wears she always wears
too little or too much
she is always too big or too small
she is always too hot or too cold
and never just right.

she wears sackcloth and ashes, goes barefoot
runs from the party at midnight
limping lopsided in a single mirrored shoe
she hides her face and buries her name
she buries her treasure.

one day she will bury her dead.

she wraps herself in scarlet
and walks into the wood to talk to wolves.
and she walks through the world

and through the stories
and she turns her unlined face towards the future
and she is young, and she is young
and she is always young.

and when she's not?

after the kissing, the dancing, the wedding

the chairs are up on the tables now
the guests have staggered home
drunk on novelty.

she's barely out of the oven
and already she's getting stale.

2: i suppose you could call this progress

stand up and walk around to the chair, pull it out and sit down at the desk, let your hands rest in front.

fx: the sound of a heartbeat fills the air. it is slow, as if you had just woken from an enchanted sleep.

>i'm 37.
>my mum died a few months ago.
>i'm told there's no right way to grieve.
>i suspect i'm doing it wrong anyway.
>i'm stressed. i'm told that:

lx: reach out and turn on the lamp. the light is white and harsh. speak evenly and calmly, as if calming a child threatening to make a fuss about a grazed knee.

>'when stressed, your menstrual cycle may become
>longer or shorter. your periods may become
>more painful or stop altogether. try to avoid
>becoming stressed by making sure you have time
>to relax. regular exercise, such as running,
>swimming and yoga, can help you relax.'

lx: turn off the lamp

>i'm 38.
>i wake up at 4am again.
>i go to work but i have to go back to check the
>door again and then i have to check the gas again
>and then i have to check the door again and then
>i have to check the gas again and then i'm late for
>work again.

fx: the heartbeat has sped up. it is now quite fast, as if you are out for a brisk walk to achieve your 10,000 recommended daily steps.

i'm 38.
a friend calls to check if i've eaten that day.
a friend takes me aside to tell me i shouldn't take it personally but i'm acting really neurotic lately and they just don't have the energy.

i'm 38.
i call at 9am but there are no free appointments this week unless it's urgent. i call at 9am but there are no free appointments this week unless it's urgent. i call at 9 am but there are no free appointments this week unless it's urgent
and i start to cry and then i can't stop. and they tell me to come in that afternoon.

fx: the heartbeat has continued to speed up. it is uncomfortably fast now, as if you are running, perhaps for an important train you are about to miss.

i'm 39.
it's my birthday
and i don't care about the numbers on the chart
and i am laughing
and i have creams to smooth my skin
and i am dancing
and i have litanies to utter on repeat
and i am drinking with my friends
and age is just a number
and i'm smiling for the photos
and the women on the tv remain in stasis

and it's a natural process
and i turn the beauty filter on my camera up
but only slightly
and nobody will guess
if i don't tell them.

i call up an old friend, tell her i've started jogging.
she laughs at me.
'oh, we're all running now', she says.
'we feel death breathing on the back of our necks
and we just start legging it'.

i'm 39.
and the doctor says he's sorry, but the second test
is definite.

fx: heatbeat stops

and the women on the tv remain in stasis
and i?

stand up

i'm running.

3. a few statistics

fx: loudly- blondie 'one way or another'

intro plays. walk around to the side of the desk. take off your outer clothing and boots to reveal running shorts and sports bra underneath. take a pair of running shoes out of the box on the floor, put them on. walk to the front of the stage.
start to run.

lx: wash fades out, spotlight fades in

blondie, sings- 'one way or another i'm gonna find you i'm gonna get ya get ya get ya get ya...'

>there are only five species of mammal known
>to experience menopause. these are the orca, the
>beluga, the short-finned pilot whale, the narwhal
>and humans.

>there are approximately 33 million humans with
>ovaries in the uk. of that group, around 13 million
>are in menopause right now and 300,000 will enter
>peri-menopause this year.

>most will experience symptoms, 25% to a severe or
>debilitating extent.

'one way or another...'

>10% report that they have considered quitting their
>jobs due to menopause symptoms.

47% report that they wouldn't feel comfortable discussing the menopause with their employer if they needed to take a day off due to symptoms.

over 50% report that the menopause has affected their sex life in a negative way.

'..i'm gonna see ya...'

hot flushes are the most common symptom of perimenopause and are reported by approximately 50%

other symptoms include:

jump

fatigue

jump

irregular periods

jump

memory loss

jump

night sweats,

jump

loss of libido

jump

vaginal dryness

jump

joint pain

jump

weight gain,

jump

hair loss

jump

mood swings

jump
      panic disorder
jump
      anxiety
jump
      insomnia
run

'...i'll get ya! i'll get ya!...'

      sleep disorders are linked to a marked decline in mental and physical health, including stress, cardiovascular disease, dementia and depression.

      according to experts, the average adult requires 7 to 9 hours sleep a night.

      according to surveys, 56% of peri-menopausal women report an average of less than 6 hours sleep a night.

      according to the app on my phone, over the last 6 months i have averaged approximately 5 hours sleep a night.

'...i'm gonna meet ya...'

      only 1% will enter peri-menopause below the age of 40. this is known as premature ovarian failure.
as well as fertility issues, people with premature ovarian failure have a higher than average risk of stress, depression, heart disease, dementia and osteoporosis.

'...one day maybe next week...'

it is strongly recommended that they take hormone replacement therapy and improve bone density by undertaking regular weightbearing or impact exercise. for example: weightlifting, aerobics, and running.

fx: soundtrack fades out

run faster

statistically, women in the uk are most likely to commit suicide between the ages of 50 and 54.

run faster

the average age of menopause is 51.

faster
faster
faster
faster
faster
faster

stop

4. definitive

lx: spot fades out, warm wash fades in centered on desk.

walk back behind the desk and sit down. your hands rest in front. your
ragged breathing cuts the flow of words.

one:

etymology: from the greek 'periodos'. originally used
in middle english to describe the time taken for an
event or incident to be completed or to end.
for example, an illness.

you didn't tell me you were leaving.
or maybe you did but not loud enough, clear enough
or you spoke in a foreign language, so i didn't
understand. i kept waiting for you.

any day now any day now any day now
...
till it was clear
you'd gone.

two:

a noun: a measure of time. for example, 'she
experienced regular periods of depression.'

if i'd have known
maybe i'd have done things differently - thrown
a party, opened a bottle of the good stuff
(red, of course).
showed my appreciation in libations and burnt

offerings, your presence sweetened by your absence
waiting
just behind the door.
but probably not.
you were always a bit of a pain and i
have always made shrines from memories.
the past is fat flickering candles; communion wafers
melting on my sacrilegious tongue
while time skips by, inhaled casually
tossed into my gasping mouth like popcorn.
slipping through my prayer-distracted hands.

three:

adjective: from or possessing typical attributes of a
bygone era. for example, 'a well preserved
period house, in need of attention'.

the door is locked now, and the doctor said
my horse had bolted long ago. i never heard
the hoofbeats. guess i wasn't listening.
maybe i thought it was rain, or distant thunder
or another nature-based symbol of my inherently
earthy feminine sensuality which is so wild it can
apparently only be properly encapsulated by a
constant flow of facebook memes featuring
mountains, sunsets, and older white women looking
pensive in autumn-coloured wool.

or maybe i had my earphones in.
deliberately.
ostentatiously.
like i do when passing building sites
or groups of men on corners.

four:

informal: added after a statement to show that any
further discussion is undesirable and will not
be entered into. for example, 'this conversation is over
now. period.'

your lack resonates
louder than that clock i never heard. i ignored
the lunar tug that snagged and caught and gradually
unravelled from inside my labyrinth
that bloody skein.
it happens. we wear down
gradually, expose the bedrock of our biology. beneath
it we are small and soft.
pale from unaccustomed light.
we curl into ourselves and squint
waiting to adjust
to the glare, the empty space.

five:

grammatical: a punctuation mark.
a full stop.

5. my darling audience

stand up

  my darling audience

fx: cue your drumroll with a gesture

  pay close attention.

  as you can see there's nothing up my sleeve, and as
  poets' wages rarely stretch to staff, i shall have to be...

*pull a red spangled leotard from the box by the desk and hold it up.
sequins catch the light - some are bent, some are missing. one of the
straps has broken and is attached with a safety-pin. there are sweat
stains under the arms.*

  ...my own glamourous assistant!

step into the leotard

  the sequins may be slightly tarnished
  but in a dim light you'll barely notice.

the zip sticks. wriggle free

  but i digress

step up onto the chair

  ladies and gentlemen, friends beyond the binary

step up onto the table

are you ready to be amazed?
are you ready for the secrets of the universe to be
unraveled?

gesture dramatically for your audience

before your very eyes?
i present to you

raise your arms

the incredible invisible woman!

as you can see, my props are minimal.
i require no bells or whistles.
i need no smoke or mirrors.
all i need is time.
all i need to do is wait.
i may seem solid now but give me another ten years
and you can watch me

fx: drumroll...

disappear.

smile

smile

nothing happens. the drumroll continues. nothing happens a bit more.
you grow slightly older. your smile grows wider and more fixed.
nothing continues to happen well past the point of awkwardness.

fx: a recorded cymbal sounds ta-da! a recorded audience applauds, rapturously.

bow. get down from the table. don't overstay your welcome.

fx: applause stops

6: a short presentation

stand in front of the desk

and now for a short presentation

pick up the presentation clicker/laser-pointer from the desk. speak clearly, precisely.

a presentation on the subject of

click. the first illustrative slide of a powerpoint presentation appears on the projector screen filling the back wall.

'things that have been in my vagina in the 9 months since diagnosis'.

click   3 sets of genital swabs and brushes.

click   4 sets of speculums, in varying sizes.

click, gesture with laser-pointer

a transducer used in the process of a transvaginal ultrasound that looked a little bit like a dildo.

click   an actual dildo.

click   lubrication to enable the entry of foreign objects into the vagina.

click   vaginal moisturiser, to be applied internally 3 times a
        week. thanks to my hrt, this is currently not necessary.
        which is nice.

click   anesthetic.

click   a syringe used to deliver the anesthetic.

click   a mirena coil inserted after the anesthetic.

click   progesterone released by the mirena coil to counter
        the increased risk of endometrial cancer caused by my
        prescribed oestrogen.

click   a nurse's fingers.

click   a consultant's fingers.

click   a doctor's fingers.

click   a different doctor's fingers.

click, wriggle fingers of right hand

        my own fingers.

        number of times i have been questioned by health care
        professionals about my recent sexual activity:

click   4

        number of times i have had my referral refused by
        the sexual health clinic because i wasn't prescribed the
        coil for purely contraceptive reasons:

click   1

number of times that i have lied to doctors at the
sexual health clinic about the frequency of my recent
sexual activity, in order to avoid being refused
treatment again, and being re-referred back to
the gynecology department of the hospital again:

click   2

number of days waiting time for an appointment at the
gynecology department of the hospital at the time of
my re-referral:

click   147

number of times i have actually engaged in sexual
activity with another human during this period:

click   0

click   thank you for your attention.

smile

turn the projector off

you can stop smiling now

7. insomnia

*turn the projector off. go back to the desk and sit down, arms resting
on the surface, hands clasped loosely in front.*
*the posture reminds you of your teacher when they said you'd be a good
student if only you'd listen more and apply yourself properly.*

lx: reach out and turn on the lamp

> 'during the course of perimenopause, your ovaries
> gradually decrease production of oestrogen as
> well as progesterone, a sleep-promoting hormone.
> this shifting of hormonal ratios can be an unsettling
> process. hot flushes and night sweats may interrupt
> sleep and frequent awakenings cause next-day fatigue.
> sleep problems are often accompanied by depression
> and anxiety. menopause-related insomnia can
> stretch on for months if not properly treated. if you're
> experiencing insomnia, you should meet with your
> doctor to discuss your options. in the meantime, try to
> relax before going to bed. yourgp may be able to
> recommend a helpful relaxation cd.'

lx: turn off the lamp

fx: wind the music box. turn the handle. listen to the lullaby

get up

turn the handle. keep playing the lullaby

take out a pillow from the box

lay out the pillow on the floor in front of the desk
keep playing the lullaby

lie down
play the lullaby

keep playing
turn the handle slower

the
turn   the   handle   slower

lullaby
stop

breathe

listen

welcome to the most relaxing way to end your day.

fx: sleep meditation music starts playing

this guided meditation is designed to help you fall
asleep, therefore never listen to this while driving or
using heavy machinery.

are you ready? let's begin.
remember that your bedroom should be a peaceful
place for rest and sleep.
temperature, lighting and noise should be controlled.
your emotions should be controlled.
do not allow yourself to feel
or appear
out of control

84

shift. get comfortable

remain calm. remain still.
allow yourself a smile.

always remember to smile.

when you're ready, simply allow your eyes to close.
begin to take deeper and slower breaths.
slower
slower
don't stop entirely though. it's important to keep on
breathing.

twist. get comfortable

imagine you're standing in front of a door. a sign on
the door reads relaxation room.
soon you'll be entering the room. soon you'll be
relaxing completely.

on the floor in front of the door is a box.
the box is designed to hold something very special.
look at the box. the box will hold all your fears and
worries and anxieties
they will flow into the box.

turn. get comfortable

you deserve to let it all go.
you deserve some time.
some of that time that you thought you had more of.
to make the decisions that have now been made for
you.

on subjects you thought you didn't care about.
can you feel it?
time, choices, chances?

shift. get comfortable

let it all go. all your fears and worries and anxieties
let them flow from deep within you down your arms
out of your fingertips and into the box.

yes. it is a very large box.

twist. get comfortable

close the lid of the box and turn your attention to the
door.
what wonderful things are behind it?
reach out, turn the doorknob, open the door.
beyond the door is a room.
the air in this room is always kept at the temperature
recommended for optimal sleep of between 18 to 24
degrees centigrade, or 60 to 67 degrees
fahrenheit depending on who you are consulting.

if your bedroom is any hotter or colder than this
then you only have yourself to blame.

in the middle of the room there is a bed.
according to the nhs uncomfortable beds are one of
the main causes of insomnia along with
recreational drugs such as ecstasy and cocaine but this
will not be a problem for you

turn. get comfortable

because the bed in the centre of this room is the most
comfortable bed.
and in any case recreational drugs are for people with
the energy to socialise.

get comfortable
get comfortable

step through the door and towards the bed
leaving the box on the floor behind you.
leave the box on the floor. don't touch the box.
definitely don't peer under the lid of the box to see
what's inside it because you know what's in
there because you just put it there.
leave the box now
don't touch the box
just don't. don't touch the box

STEP AWAY FROM THE FUCKING BOX!

fx: music stops

oh dear.
look what you've done.

clutch your pillow, crawl back under the desk

now we have to start all over again.

lie down

breathe

it's 4am, and my hormones are at it again
joyriding through my endocrine system
adrenaline surging in their wake.
my sympathetic nervous system tells me lies
tells me i'm in danger.
my body enters primal mode- asks me
what will it be - fight, or flight?

i lie in the dark, try to reason my way out of a panic
attack, try to convince my body that actually,
i'm totally safe and honestly not about to be eaten by a
sabre-tooth tiger.
but my full-throttle heart revvs against my ribs
my mouth is dry my skin slick as a seal

my body is both the kiln and the clay
and will i crack?

fx: loop pedal (will I crack?)

i don't know.
but every night i go into the furnace again, hold on and
pray for the cooling rack.

fx: looped- will i crack? will i crack? will i crack? will i...

when you wake up (when you wake up) whatever you
do don't open your eyes.
when you wake up just lie still and calm.
when you wake up just turn on the light and read.
when you wake up just get up and do something
boring, like ironing.

i don't own an iron.
so i don't have to do that one.

will i crack? will i crack? will i
　　　when you wake up when you wake up when
　　　have i tried drawing the curtains? *(have i tried drawing*
　　　the curtains) sleeping with eyemasks sleeping with
　　　earplugs sleeping with lavender under my pillow
　　　putting my pillow in the fridge using a special pillow
　　　seed cycling taking valerian magnesium herbal
　　　remedies over the counter vitamins eating less bread
　　　(eating less bread) eating less sugar eating less dairy all
　　　of which inevitably leads to me eating less altogether
　　　drinking less alcohol drinking less caffeine drinking
　　　more water but not less than three hours before bed?
　　　please try to keep up *(please try to keep up)*

will i crack? will i crack? will i
　　　wake up when you wake up when
　　　　　i tried drawing the curtains? have i tried
　　　　　　eating less bread eating less
　　　no screens in the bedroom no loud music in
　　　the bedroom no stimulation in the bedroom no fun in
　　　the bedroom.
　　　everyone
please try to keep up
　　　is very
will i crack?
　　　helpful.

fx: hit loop pedal. all sound off

crawl out from under desk
crouch on all fours

but now its 5am.
everyone tells me that blue light is evil and my phone
is basically the devil but i've waited for the dawn to
unravel so many times that the sunrise has almost
become boring and who would have thought the night
had so much time in it?

sometimes i hear cats mating. or foxes. or occasionally
my neighbours.
the foxes sound the most unhinged.

i wish i was a fox. i wish i could stand in the middle
of the road in the middle of the night and scream
and scream and scream like them.

sit back

sometimes i hear people laughing.
they pass beneath my window. heading home
from the party after the club after the bar.
the voices fade. the sky begins to pale.
the streetlights blink off. daylight swallows the stars

and nicola is online. she has been awake since 3am
and has not yet killed her husband.
he is sleeping next to her.

even his breathing is too loud, she writes.
his skin is too warm, his body is too close, the world
is too quiet and every tiny noise drops like a drum-kit
onto a concrete floor.

i've never met nicola. i don't know if i'd even like her.

i don't know how old she is, whether she is a dog
or a cat person, what sort of music she likes, whether
she voted for brexit.

she could just as well be natalie or lauren or any of
the other faceless sleepless humans sharing their lives
behind my screen, spinning their threads of
connection.

just a stranger, just one person.

sometimes that's all you need.

8. duvet days

sit cross-legged. face the projector screen on the back wall. watch the film. concentrate. don't look behind you.

> my anxiety talks to me about chaos theory
> and the butterfly effect, asks
> if i've considered all the possibilities? tells me
> fold your wings, you've no idea
> the damage you could cause, the uprooted trees
> don't care the storm was only passing through
>
> my anxiety reads the small print
> peers over my shoulder. when i turn
> we play this game: it always sidles
> out of reach, i am always
> stuck in the revolving door
>
> my anxiety says i should be prepared
> for anything, make a list: there could be bears
> between the paving cracks, a wolf on every corner
> poison apples fester in my fruit bowl
> for all i know my friends don't cast reflections
> in the mirror, in the night
> their smiles grow sharp
>
> my anxiety plants a seed. it's probably nothing.
> i fetch it a pretty pot
> we place it on my windowsill, watch it grow.
> it turns towards the sun. it fills the window frame.
> it flourishes.
> i prune it from my bed.

9. hrt

get up from the floor and sit at the desk
lx: turn the lamp on

> 'dear dr. goyder.
> katherine and i have taken some time to consider first
> of all the hormone-free alternatives to control her
> menopausal symptoms, in particular venlafaxine
> and non-hormonal osteoporosis therapy.
> however, she does appreciate that oestrogen remains
> the gold standard.'

lx: turn the lamp off
look at the box.

this is my hormone replacement therapy.

pick up the box. open it. take out a bottle. place it on the desk

the box contains one bottle of oestrogen gel and one
informative leaflet. The leaflet is quite long, and over half of it
is devoted to warnings and precautions.

take out a leaflet

the study that made everyone so scared of taking hrt is
outdated now, and apparently an equivalent risk comes from
lifestyle choices. such as drinking a lot of wine.

smooth out the creases

but still, the word cancer appears 28 times.

there's very little research into the side-effects of hrt
on people in premature menopause, so it's hard to
decide how worried to be when no one knows exactly
what the risks are.

push the leaflet to one side. it falls off the desk onto the floor

at the moment i'm settling for 'pretty worried, but
not so worried that i won't use it, because so far i've
been lucky, and all the really bad things have always
happened to other people, and if i was forced to make
a choice, like up against the wall with a gun to my
head, then i'd much rather lose my tits than my mind'.

pick up the bottle

it's best to put the gel on your skin at the same time
each day, and that bit of your skin can't touch someone
else's skin for at least an hour or your hormones will
rub off on them. the leaflet doesn't say exactly what
would happen but the implication is that it would do
strange and terrible things.

when i was little the boys in primary school used to
play a game where they'd sneak up and grab one of the
girls then run away shouting 'eeurrgh i've got girl
germs'.

push the bottle aside

as i got older i still got grabbed, they just stopped
running away. i've been groped loads by strangers in
gigs and pubs but i almost never turned round quick
enough to catch them in the act.

if my skin had purple dye in it like stolen banknotes
i could prove their guilt.

lx: lighting turns an ominous blue
lean forward

> if my life was a trashy b-movie horror film i'd rub
> hormone gel all over myself. i'd go out at night to
> contaminate those men. i'd sit in a pub and i'd wait for
> their creeping hands to touch me. i'd laugh as the
> hormones took effect and strange and terrible things
> started happening almost immediately, and as they
> fell to the floor writhing in horror the camera would
> zoom in for a close-up on my mocking smile and i'd
> ean down and I'd whisper in their dying ears

grip the desk

> you've got girl germs all over you.

sit back
lx: lighting returns to normal
smile

> don't rub the gel into your skin, instead smooth it over
> the areas and allow it to be absorbed, naturally.

> in summer it soaks in pretty quickly and i can get
> dressed straight away. in winter it takes a surprisingly
> long time to absorb. this means i end up sitting on the
> edge of the bath in my pants, shivering and waiting for
> my skin to dry.

> sometimes i just stare into space.

sometimes i stare at the goosebumps on my thighs and
wonder when the little purply veins will turn into
proper varicose veins like my mum had, and if
i'll notice the transition, or if it will be something that
someone else points out to me, like when i was told i
was now too old to walk around in public without a top
on, but not exactly why this was such a problem.

i've always quite liked my legs. they're functional, and
not so hairy that people stare at me if i wear shorts
without shaving, although i did shave in secondary
school because it's just what you did if you don't want
to be a total social outcast. i stopped when i was about
18 but it never really grew back.

it's definitely a lot easier to challenge the patriarchal
beauty constructs if nobody really notices when you're
doing it.

occasionally i do star jumps to warm up. or squats, if
i'm feeling particularly self-conscious about the shape
of my arse that morning.

usually i just look at my phone.

the adverts on my social media have changed recently.
i'm still getting all those adverts for period pants, but
now i'm also getting ones for home workouts, women's
vitamins and anti-aging serums.

fx: various women's voices

> *'...i once had a plastic surgeon who rather bluntly likened
> menopause to being akin to driving a bus into a wall, it is
> that that impactful on skin health, in terms of making it look*

classically as we associate with signs of aging...'

'...i'm talking about up here, to clear down here. wrinkled, sagging, drier...'

'...it's all gonna age, you wanna take care of your chest, and your neck, and your hands, just like you do your face, right?'

'...who wants to have a fabulous face at 58 and look like an old dinosaur everywhere else? we don't want, we don't want that.'

10. dry season

while i was travelling in australia i lived in alice springs.
it's dry season all year round there.

fx: soundtrack fades in: desert wind

during the peak of summer the river running through
town became a barren trench. i remember the parched
mud cracking, the scrubby trees clinging to the
sunbaked soil of the banks.

it's not that there's no life in a desert.
creatures still make their home there, crawl into the
dark of their dusty burrows. plants still grow.
visitors acclimatise, eventually.

but the smell when it finally rained! all the longing of
the earth for moisture filled the air, and we kicked our
trainers off and danced in the downpour.

suggested synonyms for dried include:
shriveled, parched, withered, wizened, wilted,
desiccated and arid.

i like my humour dehydrated
prefer white wine with a touch of sweetness.

i like my facts served dry but not my novels.
give me lushness, ornamentation, lift me
from the bare necessities.

i only eat dry toast when i'm ill
when nothing else stays down.

i worry that i'll dry up in the middle of a performance, that i'll forget my lines, that one day my creative juices just can't be squeezed, running out of words like a cheap biro running out of ink, and there's just no more no matter how much you shake it no matter how much you shake it there's just no more.

dried flowers are pale preserved requiems for their former selves. dairy cows are killed when their milk dries up and they cease to be productive.

fx: soundtrack fades out

it's a shame but that's the way the world is.

dried up old sticks are burnt.

fx: soundtrack fades in: natural woman by aretha franklin

pick up the pump bottle of moisturiser. apply the cream to fingers and hands, then onto arms and chest. climb up and sit on the edge of the desk to enable you to apply it more thoroughly to your thighs and shins. reach inside the leotard and apply to your breasts. allow the moisturiser to soak into the material and darken it, adding more stains. rub it all over your body, neck and face. apply with small repetitive circles over your closed eyes. sit still. keep your eyes shut. thick streaks of white smear your skin. you shine under the lights.

fx: soundtrack fades into silence

11. she used to do aerobics in the kitchen

sit up straight. open your eyes. face your audience.

mum used to do aerobics in the kitchen. she pushed
the big pine table pushed back against the wall to make
more room. she took it very seriously, followed the
women on the tv closely through a strict regime of
push-ups, sit-ups, star jumps, squats. determined to
force biology into a retreat. or at least slow it down.

she went through menopause at 42, the same age she
took up aerobics. my dad told me. when i was
diagnosed i wanted to call her up and talk but ouija
boards are notoriously unreliable and if she never felt
comfortable discussing it while she was alive i don't
see why she'd want to now she's dead. at the time it
really pissed me off. denied me a touching scene of
mother/daughter bonding. i still imagine it sometimes,
but without the awkwardness.

i've forgiven her now of course. the flood of panic has
ebbed and i'm left wandering the grubby tideline of
acceptance. you find all sorts of things poking about
around here, mud-larking. i trip over fragments of my
reflection in unexpected places.

online.
it's 5am for me
midnight for the young trans woman in the states.
our blue-lit conversation crosses oceans. we surf our
respective endocrine waves and share our hormone
rituals - both of us are on the same gel.
this aspect of our femininity comes with risks

100

we weigh them up afresh each morning

exaggerated gestures, reminiscent of a flight assistant

apply two measured pumps a day applied to upper
arms or thighs.
avoid the breast or genital area.

my grandma.
her voice wavers on the phone, pulled thin and frayed
by over 90 years of life. the conversation meanders
just passing time.
she asks me how i am. she tells me she was 40, her
husband away working and two young boys.
'it was ever so hard' she says, 'but of course, we never
talked about that then'.

in the chat groups, we talk. hundreds of us.
unseen fingers reaching out to type and tap and touch
each other's lives.

she says she feels alone.
she says she thinks she's going mad.
she says she doesn't understand the woman she's
become and neither does her husband or her friends
and her brain feels underwater and her tongue can't
make the words and she is drowning she is drowning.

and then the comments flood with tiny lifeboats.
and somewhere

she swims.

12. snip

every story has an ending - it needs one, or how would
we ever know when to look away?
we require resolution, evidence of lessons learned.
the protagonist must overcome obstacles.
the narrative arc must rise and fall, and the audience
be returned again safely.

the general outline remains the same.
the differences lie in the details, and the framing.

roll out the thread and sharpen the shears:
snip   cut here. it's a thriller,
snip   cut here. it's a romance.
snip   a tragedy.

take your pick. our fates are made to measure.
an average level of hardship comes as standard.
morals can be added for a small extra cost.

every story has a happy ending
if you chop it short enough.

i am almost 40 now.
the women on the tv remain in stasis but every month
moves me closer to the normal parameters and in ten
years' time i will seem entirely unremarkable. just
another middle-aged menopausal woman playing
grandmother's footsteps with time.

but still, let me tell you a story.

take off your shoes
> the girl wraps herself in scarlet and walks into the wood
> to talk to wolves.

take off your socks
> she tries her best to keep her knife sharp and her heart
> soft. she fills her eyes with horizons and her ears with
> others' voices.

stand up
> she walks till her shoes wear down to skin
> and her skin turns to leather.

walk forward
> she walks through the world
> and through the seasons
> and through the stories
> and she walks till she's no longer young
> and then?
>
> and then she walks some more.

turn around
walk away from the audience

lx: cut to black

walk offstage

keep walking

NOTES

after the funeral - First published in Under the Radar, issue 26, 2020

self-examination - First published in Bath Magg, issue 5, 2020

a study in vertical perspective - First published in Ink, Sweat and Tears, Oct 2020

the bear was first spotted on sunday evening - Title and first line come from environmental services official Alexander Korobkin, quoted in The Guardian, 2019: https://www.theguardian.com/world/2019/jun/18/polar-bear-russia-siberia-norilsk-climate-crisis

thoughts on forensic optography, or, 'image on her retina may show girl's slayer' - Optography is the process of retrieving and reproducing a retinal image. Forensic optography was popular in late 19th and early 20th century. It theorised that the eye recorded an image at the moment of death, and that this could be used to solve murders. Part of the title is taken from the headline of an article in the Washington Times, 1914.

what to wear when kissing girls on buses - For Melania and Chris of the 2019 London bus attack, and for everyone else whose assaults never made the headlines.

catcalled – Canto titles are taken from public advice given to women by the Metropolitan police in the wake of several different sexual assaults.

Menopause statistics and studies of gender bias in healthcare referred to are taken from various sources inc.
- https://menopausesupport.co.uk
- Lanlan Zhang, Elizabeth A. Reynolds Losin, Yoni K. Ashar, Leonie Koban, Tor D. Wager. *Gender Biases in Estimation of Others' Pain. The Journal of Pain*, 2021
- Hoffmann, Diane E. And Tarzian, Anita J., *The Girl Who Cried Pain: A Bias Against Women in the Treatment of Pain* (2001)

ACKNOWLEDGEMENTS

I did not create these poems in a vacuum. Although I've been playing with words since I was a child, this book would never have been written were it not for the support and generosity of others. From the very first time I attended a UK spoken word event in 2017, the performance poetry community has given me opportunities to try out work, spaces in which to play and dream and take risks, and the advice, critique, and inspiration I needed to progress in my craft. There are too many of you to thank individually but I will endeavor to pay it all forwards. Thanks to my publisher Verve Poetry Press for having faith in me and my work. And a huge thank you to my mentor Joelle Taylor, who told my imposter syndrome to get in the bin and helped me kick my bundle of scraggly drafts into some sort of cohesive shape. Joelle, you're a total legend and I definitely owe you a beer.

Dry Season was funded and supported by Arts Council England, with additional support from Artspace Lifespace, Bristol Old Vic Ferment, Camden People's Theatre and Apples and Snakes.

Thank you to all the women who volunteered their time and shared their menopause experiences for interviews, to my fabulous creative team and to everyone else who helped give this project shape. Laura Dannequin's invaluable dramaturgical expertise enabled me to 'put my poetry on legs' for the first time, while the experience of producers Helen Edwards and Maeve O'Neil took it out of the studio and onto the stage in front of an audience.

The incredible animation that artist and fellow poet Edalia Day created for Duvet Days led to the film being included in the official program of the 2021 Zebra Poetry Film Festival. You can watch the animation using the QR code on the next page.

Thank you to my friends who supported me through the hard times pre/post diagnosis when I was utterly miserable and more than a little mad. I love you all. Special thanks also to my then-housemate Laura Murphy, who found me crying in the kitchen shortly after my diagnosis and commiserated that yes, the situation was shit, but that it was also 'Arts Council gold' and I should think about doing something productive with it. Without her hugs, cuppas, endless encouragement and patient explanations of how to apply for funding and start to make a show, none of this would have happened.

ABOUT VERVE POETRY PRESS

Verve Poetry Press is a quite new and already award-winning press that focused initially on meeting a local need in Birmingham - a need for the vibrant poetry scene here in Brum to find a way to present itself to the poetry world via publication. Co-founded by Stuart Bartholomew and Amerah Saleh, it now publishes poets from all corners of the UK - poets that speak to the city's varied and energetic qualities and will contribute to its many poetic stories.

Added to this is a colourful pamphlet series, many featuring poets who have performed at our sister festival - and a poetry show series which captures the magic of longer poetry performance pieces by festival alumni such as Polarbear, Matt Abbott and Genevieve Carver.

The press has been voted Most Innovative Publisher at the Saboteur Awards, and has won the Publisher's Award for Poetry Pamphlets at the Michael Marks Awards.

Like the festival, we strive to think about poetry in inclusive ways and embrace the multiplicity of approaches towards this glorious art.

www.vervepoetrypress.com
@VervePoetryPres
mail@vervepoetrypress.com